# SKIING
## IN THE

### Asian Innovation

Library of Congress Cataloging-in-Publication Data

Morrison, Ian.
   Skiing in the desert : Asian Innovation / by Ian Morrison.
       p. cm. --  (Shockwave)
   Includes index.
   ISBN-10: 0-531-17583-9 (lib. bdg.)
   ISBN-13: 978-0-531-17583-5 (lib. bdg.)
   ISBN-10: 0-531-18814-0 (pbk.)
   ISBN-13: 978-0-531-18814-9 (pbk.)
   1.  Technological innovations--Asia--History--Juvenile literature.  I. Title. II. Series.

   T173.8.M665 2007
   609.5--dc22

2007022737

Published in 2008 by Children's Press, an imprint of Scholastic Inc.,
557 Broadway, New York, New York 10012
www.scholastic.com

08  09  10  11  12  13  14  15  16  17
10  9  8  7  6  5  4  3  2  1

Printed in China through Colorcraft Ltd., Hong Kong

**Author:** Ian Morrison
**Educational Consultant:** Ian Morrison
**Editor:** Lynette Evans
**Designer:** Carol Hsu
**Photo Researcher:** Jamshed Mistry

**Photographs by: AAP Image: AFP** (Chinese cupping, p. 19); AFP  **HO/Samsung Corp** (Burj tower,
p. 15); **asterweb.jpl.nasa.gov** (p. 16); **Aurora Photos/Ed Kashi/IPN** (desalination plant, p. 11);
**Courtesy of the Sharaf Group, Dubai, UAE and Iceculture, Inc., Hensall, Ontario, Canada**
(p. 30; ice restaurant, p. 31); **Getty Images** (Taipei 101, p. 15; Ocean Dome roof, p. 27; Ski
Dubai interior, p. 29; tennis court, pp. 32–33); **Jennifer and Brian Lupton** (teenagers, pp. 32–33);
**Photolibrary** (p. 14; p. 20; nanorobots, p. 21); **Stock Central/TopFoto** (Ocean Dome, interior
view, p. 27); **Stock X.chng** (p. 34); **Tranz: Corbis** (p. 8; visually impaired students, solar energy
panels, p. 11; p. 18; weighing herbs, pp. 18–19; pp. 22–24; boy with kite, p. 25; p. 26; p. 28; ice
sculpture, p. 31); **Reuters** (cover; p. 7; nanotechnician, p. 21; fireworks, p. 25); **Rex Features** (p. 3;
p. 17; Ski Dubai exterior, p. 29)

The publisher would like to thank Julian Bayley of Iceculture Inc. for the photos of the ice
restaurant on pages 30–31.

SHOCKWAVE
SCIENCE

# SKIING
## IN THE
# DESERT

## Asian Innovation

Ian Morrison

**children's press**®

An imprint of Scholastic Inc.

NEW YORK • TORONTO • LONDON • AUCKLAND • SYDNEY
MEXICO CITY • NEW DELHI • HONG KONG
DANBURY, CONNECTICUT

# CHECK THESE OUT!

**SHOCKER**

Stuff to Shock,
Surprise, and
Amaze You

Quick Recaps
and Notable
Notes

Word Stunners
and Other Oddities

The Heads-Up
on Expert Reading

Links to More
Information

# CONTENTS

**artificial** (*ar ti FISH uhl*) produced by humans, not natural

**chemotherapy** the treatment of cancer using a mixture of chemicals or drugs

**continent** one of the seven main land masses on the earth

**cyber** controlled by or having to do with a computerized system

**heritage** valued traditions handed down from generation to generation

**innovation** (*in uh VAY shuhn*) a new idea or an improvement to an existing invention

**retractable** (*ree TRAKT uh buhl*) able to be pulled  back, or in

**symmetrical** having formal balance in relation to an axis or central point

For additional vocabulary, see Glossary on page 34.

The word *cyber* is a shortened version of *cybernetics*. This word was first used in English in the 1940s. Other related words include: *cyberspace*, *cybercafé*, and *cyborg* (a combination of the words *cybernetic* and *organism*).

A huge automated roof can be opened or closed over the world's largest indoor water park, in Japan.

In what part of the world have people built high-rise cities and snow-covered mountains in the middle of scorching desert sands? Where is the longest human-made structure on the planet? Where was the world's first bicycle-riding robot manufactured? And where is the earth's largest indoor water park? In Asia, that's where.

Asia is the largest of the world's seven **continents**. It stretches from Africa and Europe in the west to the Pacific Ocean in the east. In parts of Asia, desert stretches as far as the eye can see. Some parts of Asia lie in the frozen Arctic. Other parts lie in the tropics.

A businessman looks out over construction taking place in the central business district of Dubai, United Arab Emirates (UAE).

More than 60 percent of the world's population lives in Asia. There are 50 countries in all. The total population is about four billion people. China is the world's most heavily populated country, with more than 1.3 billion people. More than 1.1 billion people live in India. Asia is home to the world's most ancient civilizations. The people of Asia have a long history of invention and **innovation**. Today, Asia continues to make huge contributions in many areas of science and technology.

■ **Asia**

Arctic Ocean

Russia

EUROPE

Kazakhstan

Mongolia

**ASIA**

Turkey

Japan

Israel

Iraq

Iran

China

South Korea

AFRICA

Saudi Arabia

United Arab Emirates

India

Taiwan

Pacific Ocean

Indian Ocean

Malaysia

Indonesia

**KEY TO CLIMATE**

| | | | |
|---|---|---|---|
| ■ **Polar** | ■ **Mountain temperate** | ■ **Desert and semidesert** | ■ **Subtropical** |
| ■ **Cold temperate** | ■ **Dry temperate** | ■ **Wet temperate** | ■ **Tropical** |

# PROBLEM SOLVERS – PAST AND PRESENT

Many people think of Asia as a place of traditional values. It is a continent rich in ancient customs and **heritage**. Perhaps unfairly, Asia has been known more for its cultural than for its scientific advances. However, many of the tools and technologies we use today were invented long ago in Asia. People in parts of ancient Asia led the way in inventing practical ways to solve problems. From coins to compasses, from wheelbarrows to water pumps, many early Asian inventions have made a huge difference to the world.

Today, people in Asia continue to be as innovative as ever. They make fresh water from the salty sea. They build islands in the ocean. They put snow in the desert. They are leading the way in computer and robotic technologies. They are providing solutions to overcrowding, disease, energy needs, transportation, communication, and climate challenges.

## Time Line of Early Inventions From Asia

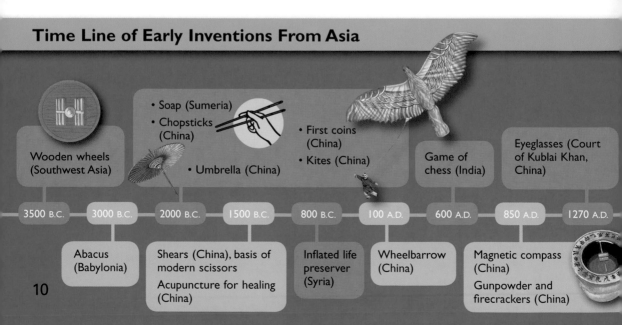

Wooden wheels (Southwest Asia)

• Soap (Sumeria)
• Chopsticks (China)

• Umbrella (China)

• First coins (China)
• Kites (China)

Game of chess (India)

Eyeglasses (Court of Kublai Khan, China)

| 3500 B.C. | 3000 B.C. | 2000 B.C. | 1500 B.C. | 800 B.C. | 100 A.D. | 600 A.D. | 850 A.D. | 1270 A.D. |

Abacus (Babylonia)

Shears (China), basis of modern scissors

Acupuncture for healing (China)

Inflated life preserver (Syria)

Wheelbarrow (China)

Magnetic compass (China)

Gunpowder and firecrackers (China)

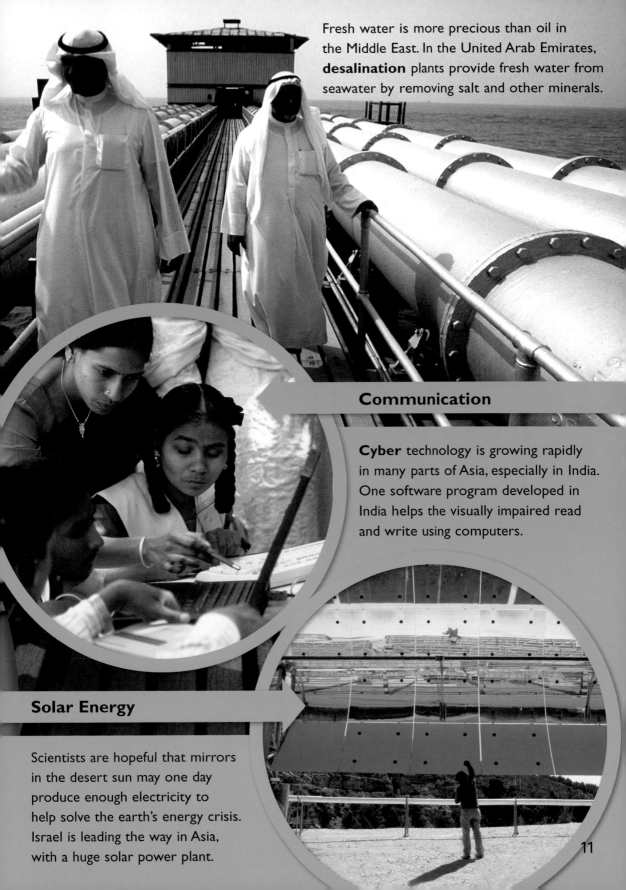

Fresh water is more precious than oil in the Middle East. In the United Arab Emirates, **desalination** plants provide fresh water from seawater by removing salt and other minerals.

## Communication

**Cyber** technology is growing rapidly in many parts of Asia, especially in India. One software program developed in India helps the visually impaired read and write using computers.

## Solar Energy

Scientists are hopeful that mirrors in the desert sun may one day produce enough electricity to help solve the earth's energy crisis. Israel is leading the way in Asia, with a huge solar power plant.

11

## GREAT WALLS AND PRICELESS PALACES

Asian engineers have always excelled in the building of spectacular structures. Many of these marvels were completed thousands of years ago. They were constructed long before the invention of modern machines and computer-aided engineering.

The most gifted scientists, mathematicians, and craftspeople were involved in designing and building these amazing structures. Some of these structures can still be visited today. The Taj Mahal in India and the Great Wall in China are two examples of early Asian construction and technology.

I remember seeing a documentary on TV about the Great Wall of China. Knowing something about it already made me interested to read more about it.

Parts of the Great Wall of China were built about 2,000 years ago to keep out invaders. The wall stretches some 4,500 miles across northern China. It is still the world's longest human-made structure.

The Taj Mahal, in India, was built between 1630 and 1650, using 22,000 workers. The Indian emperor Shah Jahan ordered the magnificent tomb to be built in honor of his wife. The building and the gardens around it are perfectly **symmetrical**.

The Taj Mahal is made entirely of marble. The marble was cut and fitted together like pieces of a puzzle.

SHOCKER

More than 1,000 elephants were used to transport heavy building materials to the Taj Mahal site.

The Taj Mahal was designed by a Turkish architect. Palaces in the East were often decorated with beautiful carvings, **mosaics**, and tiles. Since ancient times, craftspeople from the Middle East have made tiles from baked clay.

13

# BUILDING UP

Asia has more than half the world's population. However, there is little suitable land to build on. One solution is to build upward. People in Asia have developed the skills and technology necessary to build super skyscrapers. Until recently, these buildings were often associated with western cities. They are now springing up all over Asia.

In 1998, Malaysia celebrated the completion of the Petronas Towers in Kuala Lumpur. At the time, they were the world's tallest buildings. However, five years later, in Taipei, Taiwan, an even taller building went up. Taipei 101 was completed in 2003. It is now the tallest building in the world. But it won't be the tallest for long! A super-tall skyscraper, the Burj, is under construction in Dubai. The Burj will be the tallest self-standing structure in the world. It is expected to be at least 1,375 feet higher than the Empire State Building! However, the final height of this supertower is a closely kept secret.

**Petronas Towers**

The 88-story Petronas Towers are joined at the 42nd floor by a skybridge. This $1.6-billion complex even has room for 4,500 cars in its underground parking lot!

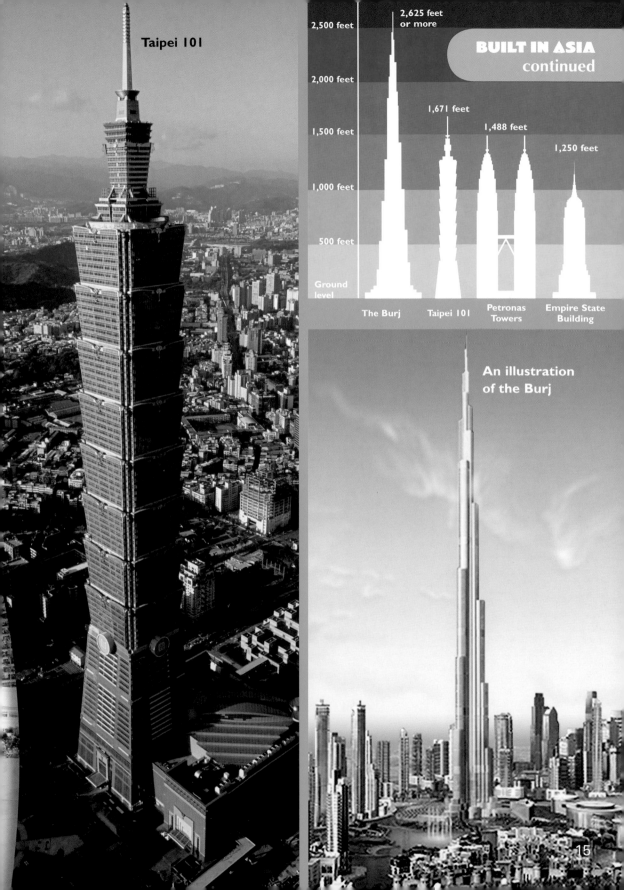

**Taipei 101**

2,500 feet

2,000 feet

1,500 feet

1,000 feet

500 feet

Ground level

2,625 feet or more

1,671 feet

1,488 feet

1,250 feet

The Burj | Taipei 101 | Petronas Towers | Empire State Building

**An illustration of the Burj**

15

# BUILDING OUT

Dubai is a city in the United Arab Emirates. In just 50 years, it has been transformed from a quiet village to an ultramodern urban center. Building upward is only one of the solutions to this rapid growth. Dubai is now building where no land exists! Three huge **artificial** islands are being constructed off the coast. These are known as the Palm Islands. Each island is in the shape of a palm tree.

The first island, Palm Jumeirah, is home to more than 60,000 people. It has 32 hotels and hundreds of stores. Residents have all the advantages of a modern city, while being steps away from their very own beach. Palm Jumeirah is small compared to the other two islands. When the third island, Palm Deira, is finished, it will be larger than the city of Paris!

**Palm Jebel Ali**

**Palm Jumeirah**

**The World**
**(under construction)**

**Palm Deira**
**(under construction)**

A fourth project is called "The World." A total of 300 islands will be built in the shape of the continents of the world. Some will have private homes. Others will be **resorts**.

Palm Jumeirah

## Creative Solutions

**Problem**: a large population and very little land

**Solution**: building up or building out

## Building an Island

Sand

Each island is constructed from sand taken from the Persian Gulf. A **breakwater** of rocks needs to be placed around the island. There are more than 14,000 laborers working around the clock to build these artificial islands.

17

# MEDICAL MARVELS

More than 2,000 years ago, doctors in ancient China used herbs and special healing methods to cure disease and to keep people healthy. Traditional Chinese medicine (TCM) is sometimes called an **alternative** medicine by people in the western world. It involves the use of herbs, **acupuncture**, and physical therapy. Many doctors in the West have looked upon TCM as unproven and unscientific. However, attitudes are beginning to change. Western doctors and scientists are now looking more closely at the use of TCM. It appears that TCM may be more beneficial than they once thought.

Many western medical schools now include alternative medicine in some of their classes. Drug companies are beginning to recognize the value of traditional medicines. Doctors are experimenting with TCM for pain relief. It is hoped that TCM can help ease some of the worst side effects of **chemotherapy** in cancer patients.

## Getting the Point

Acupuncture involves inserting and manipulating needles in specific points of the body. It is used mainly for treating pain. It is also believed to restore a feeling of well-being.

Plants are an important ingredient in Chinese medicines. People often drink herbs in teas. Doctors prescribe **remedies** that mix the leaves, roots, and barks of various plants.

## Traditional Chinese Medicine

- uses herbs, acupuncture, and physical therapy
- is used to relieve pain
- is believed to relieve some side effects of chemotherapy
- is becoming more accepted in the West

## Sucked In

An ancient Chinese healing technique called cupping is becoming more common in western medicine today. Heated suction cups are used to relieve muscle pain and improve circulation.

19

# TECH TALK

# NANOTECHNOLOGY

Nanotechnology is a revolutionary area of research. It deals with things that are too small to see. Nanotech scientists are working on technology that will allow tiny robots to target and destroy cancer cells in the body. They are also developing **sensors** made up of nanowires that will detect early signs of cancer. Someday, surgeons may even use nanotechnology to reconnect tissue during surgery.

Nano-sized objects are very, very tiny. Scientists are becoming skilled at manipulating tiny bits of **matter** to make new products. They can make microscopic tools. They are creating products that are cleaner, lighter, and stronger. Japan is emerging as a world leader in this field.

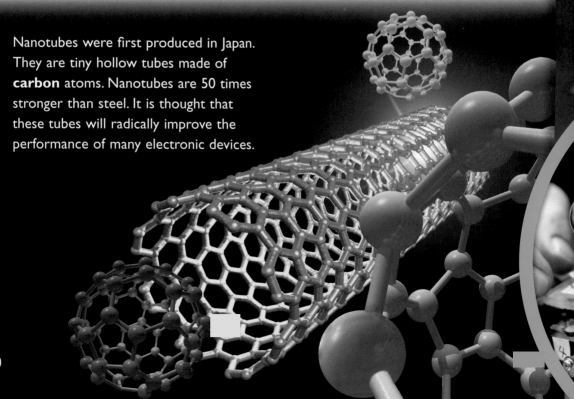

Nanotubes were first produced in Japan. They are tiny hollow tubes made of **carbon** atoms. Nanotubes are 50 times stronger than steel. It is thought that these tubes will radically improve the performance of many electronic devices.

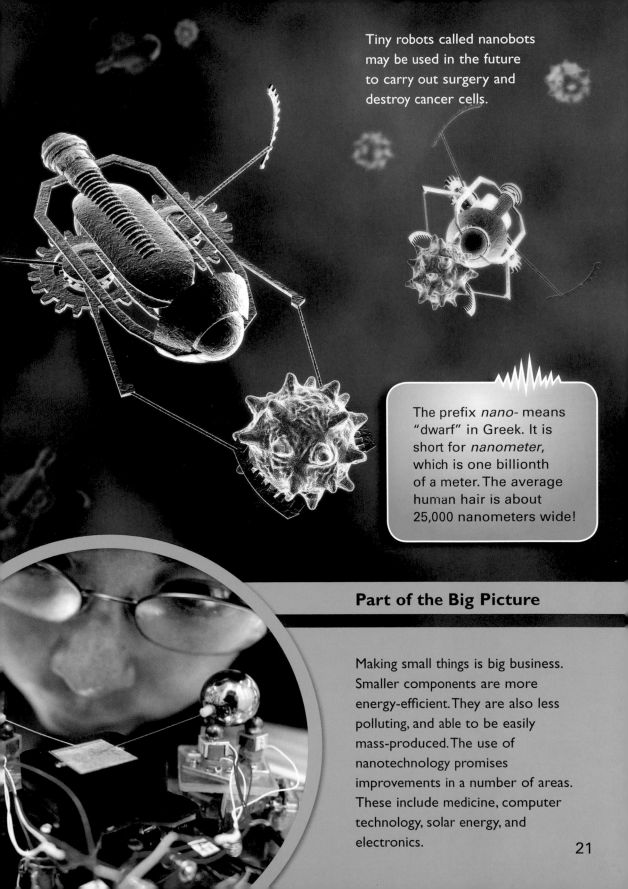

Tiny robots called nanobots may be used in the future to carry out surgery and destroy cancer cells.

The prefix *nano-* means "dwarf" in Greek. It is short for *nanometer*, which is one billionth of a meter. The average human hair is about 25,000 nanometers wide!

## Part of the Big Picture

Making small things is big business. Smaller components are more energy-efficient. They are also less polluting, and able to be easily mass-produced. The use of nanotechnology promises improvements in a number of areas. These include medicine, computer technology, solar energy, and electronics.

21

# ROBOT REVOLUTION

Robots are high-tech machines that have computers for brains. They are programmed with instructions and wired with a network of electronic sensors. Robots have helped make life easier for humans for decades. Some do difficult and dangerous work. Some are interactive toys that can walk, talk, and play. Some help in homes and hospitals. Some are designed to look and move like humans.

Robots are still a long way from being human-like. However, the technology is constantly being improved. Japan is a pioneer in this field. Some engineers are creating superbots. These robots can transform into different shapes for different tasks.

> That was really funny! I just misread the word "wired." I thought it was "weird." As I continued reading, it made no sense. So I went back and thought, "What word would make sense, sound right, and look right?" The word was *wired*, of course!

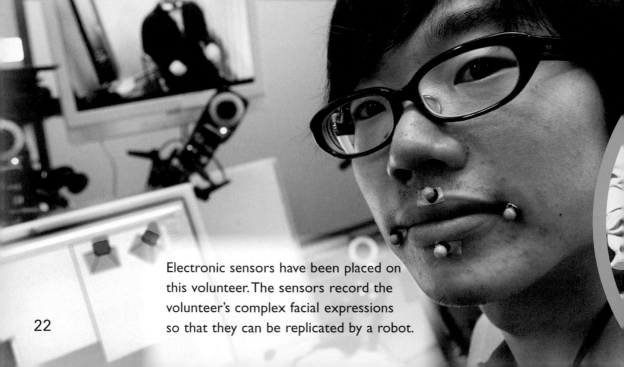

Electronic sensors have been placed on this volunteer. The sensors record the volunteer's complex facial expressions so that they can be replicated by a robot.

Murata Boy is the world's first bicycle-riding robot. It was made in Tokyo, Japan.

## Cyber Scene

Information technology and engineering are huge industries in India. India is leading the world in many areas of software development. Some companies finance and operate community programs. They donate computers to schools. They also help educate people in villages about computer technology.

23

# FUN AND GAMES

Many forms of entertainment enjoyed around the world today began in Asia. Kites first appeared in China more than 2,500 years ago. At first, kites were used for more than fun and games. People in China believed that they would scare away evil spirits. They also used them to keep birds away from crops. Kite flying was soon introduced to Japan. Builders there had the good idea of using kites to help them lift tiles onto the roofs of houses. Large kites were even used to lift people off the ground. In Indonesia, fishermen suspended their fishing lines from kites made of woven palm leaves.

Since early on, kites have been used for scientific purposes. In 1752, Benjamin Franklin used a kite to experiment with electricity. He was lucky not to be **electrocuted**. In 1901, a kite was used to carry a radio receiver into the sky over part of Canada. From the receiver on that kite, the first radio signals were **transmitted** across the Atlantic Ocean. Kites were also used to carry weather instruments to great altitudes.

People around the world enjoy playing chess. Historians believe that the game began in India in around 600 A.D.

Kite flying is a tradition in Afghanistan. It is so popular that it is almost a national sport.

## Fire in the Sky

The fireworks displays we enjoy today originated in China. The ancient Chinese invented gunpowder to make firecrackers. Firecrackers were believed to scare away evil spirits. Today, fireworks displays are enjoyed by people throughout the world.

# INDOOR SURFING

If flying a kite or watching a fireworks display isn't your thing, why not try indoor surfing? Imagine lying on a beach under a perfect blue sky. The water is always warm. There is absolutely no chance of a shark attack. It's never going to rain, because this scene is all indoors!

Ocean Dome in Japan is the world's largest indoor water park. It is covered by a 260-foot **retractable** roof. The beach is made of 600 tons of polished marble chips. You can lie on the beach and read a book. You can ride the gentle waves on your boogie board. Or you can watch the experts surf the 11-foot waves. There is even an artificial volcano that erupts every hour!

SHOCKER

Although Ocean Dome is located close to a pleasant sandy beach with good surf, the real beach is nearly always deserted!

gentle waves

perfect blue
sky

water always
warm

**Ocean Dome
selling points**

no chance
of rain

attractive
marble sand

no shark
attacks!

## World's Largest Retractable Roof

Rain is never a problem for
swimmers and surfers at
Ocean Dome. When the huge
retractable roof slides shut, its
cloud-streaked, blue-sky ceiling
is a close imitation of nature.

27

# SKIING IN THE DESERT

When it comes to re-creating nature's wonders, engineers in Dubai have put imagination and technology to work in a very big way. They have built mountains where there was once desert. They have created snow to replace hot sand. Dubai has built a 25-story, snow-covered mountain with ski slopes. This artificial mountain has been placed inside the world's third largest mall!

In Dubai, the temperature is often in the high 90s. Imagine being able to cool off and have fun at the same time. At Ski Dubai, visitors have a choice of five ski runs. Winter clothing, ski boots, skis, and snowboards are supplied. There are even chairlifts to carry skiers up the mountain. Patrollers make sure skiers stay safe.

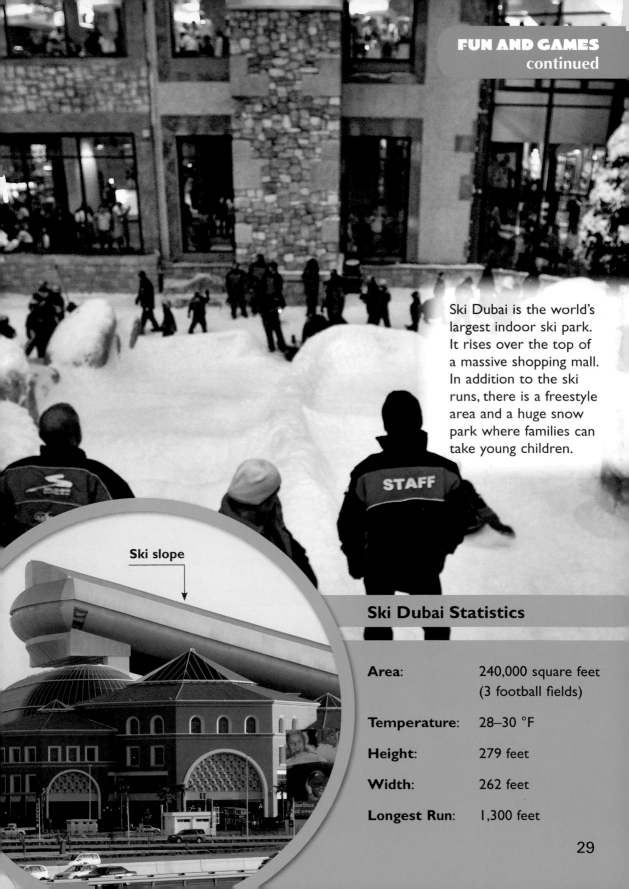

Ski Dubai is the world's largest indoor ski park. It rises over the top of a massive shopping mall. In addition to the ski runs, there is a freestyle area and a huge snow park where families can take young children.

Ski slope

## Ski Dubai Statistics

| | |
|---|---|
| **Area**: | 240,000 square feet (3 football fields) |
| **Temperature**: | 28–30 °F |
| **Height**: | 279 feet |
| **Width**: | 262 feet |
| **Longest Run**: | 1,300 feet |

29

# CHILLING OUT

When summer strikes in Dubai, chilling out is all most people can think about. Perhaps that's why this city is home to the world's first all-ice restaurant. The temperatures inside are at chilly, sub-arctic levels. Diners sit on ice chairs at ice tables. They eat from ice plates and drink from ice glasses. Ice sculptures of Dubai's city highlights are on display. The furniture and sculptures may last as long as eight months before losing their shape. However, they are changed every three months to keep people interested and entertained. Diners are given warm jackets, gloves, and shoes for their chilly eating experience. But the meal needs to be a fast one. Unless you are a polar bear, the recommended stay is just 40 minutes!

As soon as I read the word *Dubai* in the first sentence, I made the connection to what I had already read about that place. I just knew these pages would contain something spectacular, and I wasn't disappointed!

Highly skilled ice artists create a magical world of ice carvings for display in Dubai.

## Ice in the Desert

More than 45 tons of ice were used to build the ice restaurant. The ice was cut, carved, then shipped in freezer containers from Canada to Dubai. Storing ice in the desert heat is not a new technique. In ancient Iran, engineers built underground chambers cooled by a system of wind-catchers. Ice was brought from the mountains and served as a royal summer treat.

31

Huge complexes like Ocean Dome and Ski Dubai cost a great deal of money to build and operate. They consume massive amounts of energy. A lot of this energy is generated by **nonrenewable resources**, such as oil. Some parts of Asia are rich in oil reserves. These places have a wealthy economy. They can add to this by creating unique complexes that attract visitors from around the world.

## WHAT DO YOU THINK?

Should people be allowed to provide entertainment that uses a lot of nonrenewable energy?

### PRO

People should be able to have whatever type of entertainment they wish. If they are paying for it, it should be their choice. Running out of energy is not a problem. By the time we begin to run out, scientists will have developed ways to use wind, solar, and tidal energy to provide all the energy people need.

Playing tennis in the snow at Ski Dubai

Nature provides many forms of entertainment for free. Traditional activities, such as kite flying, skipping rope, or ball sports are inexpensive. They use renewable forms of energy, such as wind and muscle power. People in many parts of Asia struggle to meet even the basic needs of food, shelter, and education. They have little opportunity for the luxury of fun and games.

## CON

The earth's resources belong to everyone. Just because some people have money, they shouldn't feel entitled to waste resources. If people want to surf or ski, they should take a trip to the seaside or to the mountains. Wealthy nations could make extra money available to help people who are struggling.

# GLOSSARY

**acupuncture** (*AK yoo pungk chur*) a way of treating illness by pricking specific parts of the body with small needles

**alternative** (*ahl TUR nuh tiv*) different from what is usual

**breakwater** a wall built to protect a harbor or beach from the force of ocean waves

**carbon** a chemical element found in all plants and animals

**desalination** (*dee sal uh NAY shun*) the process of changing salt water into fresh water

**electrocute** (*i LEK truh kyoot*) to injure or kill yourself or someone else with a severe electric shock

**matter** a substance; any solid, liquid, or gas

**mosaic** (*moh ZAY ik*) a picture or pattern made up of different-colored pieces of tiles, stones, or glass

**nonrenewable resource** something used to make energy that is not replaceable after having been used, such as oil and coal

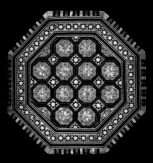

**Mosaic**

**remedy** (*REM uh dee*) something that relieves pain, cures a disease, or corrects a disorder

**resort** (*ri ZORT*) a place where people go for rest and relaxation

**sensor** (*SEN sur*) an instrument that responds to or detects heat, sound, or pressure

**transmit** to send a signal by wire or radio waves

# FIND OUT MORE

## BOOKS

Donovan, Sue. *Istanbul: Once Constantinople*. Scholastic Inc., 2008.

Hosking, Wayne. *Asian Kites*. Tuttle Publishing, 2004.

Johnson, Rebecca L. *Nanotechnology*. Lerner Publishing, 2005.

Mann, Elizabeth. *The Great Wall: The Story of 4,000 Miles of Earth and Stone That Turned a Nation Into a Fortress*. Mikaya, 2006.

Oxlade, Chris. *Skyscrapers: Uncovering Technology*. Firefly Books, 2006

Tagliaferro, Linda and Brown, Stephen F. *Taj Mahal: India's Majestic Tomb*. Bearport Publishing, 2005.

## WEB SITES

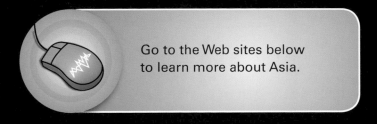

Go to the Web sites below
to learn more about Asia.

www.petronastwintowers.com.my

www.enchantedlearning.com/subjects/greatwall

www.pbs.org/treasuresoftheworld/taj_mahal/tmain.html

www.skidxb.com

# INDEX

# ABOUT THE AUTHOR

Ian Morrison is the author of a number of books for children and teachers. Before becoming a full-time writer, he taught elementary school for many years, worked with children with reading difficulties, and trained teachers and reading specialists. Ian and his wife live in New Zealand and love to travel. Asia is a favorite destination. They love the mix of the very old with cutting-edge technology that can be found in Asia. And that is what *Skiing in the Desert* is all about.